Original title:
The Journey to Us

Copyright © 2024 Swan Charm
All rights reserved.

Author: Sebastian Sarapuu
ISBN HARDBACK: 978-9916-89-625-9
ISBN PAPERBACK: 978-9916-89-626-6
ISBN EBOOK: 978-9916-89-627-3

Crossing Unseen Boundaries

We walk our paths in silence,
Each step a whispered dream.
Unseen threads connect our hearts,
Crossing boundaries that gleam.

In the shadows where we tread,
Fears and hopes intertwine.
Together we brave the unknown,
In a dance of fate divine.

The world expands in our embrace,
Wonders bloom where we care.
With courage, we lift the veil,
Discovering treasures rare.

With every shared secret shared,
A bond is forged anew.
Crossing unseen boundaries,
Our spirits journey through.

Together we build a canvas,
Colors of joy and pain.
In unity, we find our voice,
A harmony that remains.

Rivers of Shared Experience

Flowing through the valleys deep,
Rivers carry tales untold.
Shared experiences like currents,
In their depths, we're bold.

Together we navigate the bends,
Where laughter greets the night.
The waters shimmer with our stories,
In a dance of pure delight.

Bridges form with every word,
Connecting hearts in trust.
In the flow of time and space,
We find the strength we must.

As we drift along the banks,
The journey is our creed.
In the rivers of experience,
We plant the seeds we need.

Together we'll forge memories,
In the tides that shape our way.
A landscape rich with purpose,
In the light of each new day.

Reflections on Shared Paths

Amidst the trees, we wander near,
Paths entwined, our spirits soar.
Reflections dance upon the leaves,
Echoes of what came before.

In the twilight's gentle glow,
Memories twinkle, soft and bright.
Together we chart our journeys,
In the canvas of the night.

Every step an affirmation,
Of bonds both deep and true.
We gather moments like petals,
In the garden we construe.

Whispers of the wind remind,
Of laughter shared in trust.
On these paths, we shape our fate,
In unity, we must.

As dawn unfolds with promise,
Another chapter starts anew.
Reflections on the paths we take,
Together, me and you.

Alchemy of Hearts

In the crucible of our dreams,
We blend our hopes and fears.
Alchemy transforms our wounds,
Into wisdom through the years.

With every challenge faced as one,
We forge an iron will.
The magic of our shared resolve,
Breathes strength when time stands still.

Threads of kindness weave a tapestry,
Vivid hues of grace.
In the alchemy of our hearts,
We find our sacred space.

Through storms and calm, we venture,
With hearts that shine like gold.
In the furnace of our togetherness,
Love's true stories unfold.

In the dance of fate, we gather,
Moments precious and bright.
In this alchemy of hearts,
We create our shared light.

Voices of Shared Experience

In the quiet of the night,
Whispers float like gentle breeze.
Stories shared under the stars,
Unite us in our ease.

Through laughter and through tears,
We weave the threads of fate.
Bound by joys and sorrows,
Together we navigate.

In the warmth of friendly eyes,
We find solace and strength.
Echoes of our journeys,
Resonating at great length.

With every step we take,
Our souls begin to blend.
In the tapestry of time,
We discover a friend.

And as the dawn breaks forth,
Each voice lifts like a song.
Together we embrace the light,
In unity, we belong.

Through the Lenses of Love

A gaze that speaks a thousand words,
In silence, hearts entwine.
Moments caught like fireflies,
Illumined paths align.

Through trials and through laughter,
Our spirits rise and soar.
With every shared adventure,
We cherish even more.

Hands clasped in tender trust,
We face what lies ahead.
Each heartbeat echoes softly,
In love, we are led.

With dreams that intertwine,
Together we explore.
Through the lenses of our hearts,
We find the open door.

In every whispered promise,
A landscape of our own.
A world created just for us,
Where love has overthrown.

Gardens of Possibility

Seeds of hope lie dormant,
In fertile grounds of chance.
With patience and with care,
We tend to each new glance.

Buds begin to blossom,
Colors burst into view.
With every ray of sunlight,
Our dreams start to break through.

In the garden of our hearts,
We plant with tender hands.
Nurturing together,
We cultivate our plans.

With winds of change a-blowing,
We watch our visions grow.
In the soil of our passions,
Endless pathways will show.

And as the seasons shift,
New possibilities arise.
In this garden we create,
We embrace the boundless skies.

Interwoven Destinies

Like threads upon a loom,
Our lives entwined with grace.
Each twist and turn reveals,
A shared and sacred space.

In the fabric of our days,
We find strength in the blend.
Together, we create,
A story without end.

Through storms that come our way,
We stand side by side.
In unity, we flourish,
Our destinies collide.

With every step we take,
New patterns come to light.
In the tapestry of time,
We share the warmth of night.

And when we look back fondly,
At the paths we've carved with care,
We see the art of living,
In the love we choose to share.

Constellations of Us

In the night, we shine bright,
Connecting stars, our shared light.
Whispers of dreams in the dark,
Guided by love, we embark.

Each moment, a spark ignites,
Drawing us close on starry nights.
In silence, our hearts converse,
A universe woven through verse.

The map of souls, vast and wide,
In constellations, we confide.
Galaxies dance, a cosmic sway,
Together we'll find our way.

Through storms that may shake our core,
We soar high, forevermore.
In the canvas of endless skies,
Together, we rise and rise.

In the tapestry of fate,
We create. We celebrate.
Each star a story, bold and true,
Constellations of me and you.

Embracing the Unknown

The road ahead is veiled in mist,
Yet we venture, hands entwined, kissed.
With every step, our fears we face,
In the unknown, we find our place.

Whispers of doubts fade in the light,
Hope guides us through the darkest night.
With courage steeped in dreams we weave,
Together, we learn to believe.

In the shadows, new paths await,
Exploring moments we create.
With open hearts, we greet the day,
Embracing chaos on our way.

Waves of change may rise and fall,
Yet in your presence, I stand tall.
Every twist, a chance to grow,
In the unknown, our spirits flow.

Let's dance beneath the stars above,
In the silence, we find our love.
Through every twist, we shall endure,
Embracing all, steadfast and sure.

Wings of Unity

Together we rise, side by side,
With wings of unity, we glide.
In harmony, our hearts align,
Through every storm, your hand in mine.

Across the skies, we build our dreams,
Flowing like rivers, merging streams.
Bound by love, we touch the skies,
On whispered winds, our spirits rise.

In every color, we find our voice,
Painting the world, we rejoice.
In this journey, we're never alone,
With wings of unity, we've grown.

Through trials faced, we learn to soar,
Finding strength in what we adore.
Together we'll write our tale,
With love as our wind-filled sail.

In the dance of life, we are free,
With you, my heart embraces glee.
Together we'll journey, hand in hand,
On wings of unity, we'll stand.

Harmonies of Time

In the symphony of days gone by,
Each note a memory, a gentle sigh.
Time flows like rivers, deep and wide,
In harmonies, we find our guide.

Moments echo, sweet and clear,
In laughter and joy, we hold dear.
Through the seasons, our song remains,
Melodies rise, life's sweet refrains.

Gathered together, hearts entwined,
In the rhythms of life, we're aligned.
With every heartbeat, a story told,
In the harmonies, our souls unfold.

As dawn greets the fading night,
We dance through shadows into light.
In paths of time that intertwine,
We blossom, forever divine.

In the tapestry woven through years,
Our laughter, our love, our shared tears.
Together, we cherish the climb,
Creating our own harmonies of time.

A World Within Us

In whispers deep, our secrets dwell,
A universe that time can't quell.
Each heartbeat sings, a gentle tune,
A symphony beneath the moon.

Dreams awaken in shadows cast,
Memories linger, futures vast.
Through silent echoes, we must roam,
To find the strength that leads us home.

Mountains rise in every heart,
Yet valleys wide, they play their part.
We navigate both joy and pain,
Through storms of life, we learn to reign.

A garden grows in thoughts we sow,
In every doubt, a seed to grow.
With open minds, we seek the light,
In the darkness, we find our sight.

United voices, a chorus strong,
Together we find where we belong.
In our hearts, a world unfolds,
A tapestry of dreams retold.

Finding Our North Star

Beneath the vast, unending sky,
We search for truths that never lie.
With every step, we chart our course,
Guided by hope, a gentle force.

Winds may shift, but still we sail,
Each choice we make tells our own tale.
Stars above gleam, a map so bright,
In darkest hours, they shine their light.

With courage stitched in every seam,
We stitch together every dream.
Through valleys deep and mountains tall,
Together we rise, together we fall.

A compass forged from love and trust,
In every journey, it's a must.
As paths converge, we start to see,
The North Star shines, our destiny.

With hands held tight, we find our way,
Through night and day, come what may.
In unity, our spirits soar,
Finding the star that guides us more.

Stories Carved in Sand

Waves embrace the shoreline's edge,
Where footprints fade, a timeless pledge.
Each grain of sand, a tale unfolds,
In whispers soft, the ocean holds.

Seashells whisper, secrets kept,
In tide's embrace, where dreams are slept.
Each ebb and flow, a memory spins,
The dance of life, where loss begins.

Hearts grow heavy, carried by tide,
In fleeting moments, we confide.
Yet with the dawn, hope's glow returns,
For every loss, a lesson learns.

Time washes clean the jagged line,
That marks the spots where we align.
With patience, we await the rise,
Of new horizons, endless skies.

So let us write our stories bold,
In every wave, in every fold.
With laughter, love, and sunlit land,
Our lives are tales, like stories carved in sand.

As We Walk, We Become

With every step along this road,
We find ourselves, take on the load.
Each path we tread, a new embrace,
In every stranger, a familiar face.

Moments linger, a fleeting glance,
In times of quiet, we take a chance.
With open hearts, we learn to see,
That every journey sets us free.

Together we weave our stories tight,
In daylight's grace and starry night.
As we walk, the world unfolds,
A dance of tales yet to be told.

With minds unguarded, we explore,
The beauty found in every door.
Each connection softens the ache,
In our shared steps, new memories wake.

As seasons change, we grow and bend,
In every heartbeat, a new friend.
With every journey, love's design,
As we walk together, we define.

Dances Beneath the Moonlight

Under silver beams we sway,
Whispers of night guide our way.
In the glow, shadows twirl free,
Glances exchanged, just you and me.

The stars, they wink, a playful tease,
Rustling leaves accompany the breeze.
Footprints left in soft, warm sand,
Wrapped in magic, hand in hand.

The night unfolds like velvet dreams,
Laughter echoes, or so it seems.
A symphony of heartbeats race,
In this moment, we find our place.

As the moon dips low, we slow our pace,
Time stands still, a gentle grace.
With every spin, the world fades out,
In our hearts, there lies no doubt.

For beneath this sky, so vast and bright,
We dance together, lost in light.
Forever etched in memory's frame,
Dances beneath the moonlight's name.

The Map of Our Souls

In the depths of whispered dreams,
We trace the lines, a silent scheme.
Stars are markers, guiding our way,
Through winding paths where shadows play.

Each heartbeat speaks a secret truth,
The map unfolds, revealing youth.
Across the valleys, mountains so tall,
In the silence, we hear the call.

With every step, we venture deep,
Into the memories we choose to keep.
X marks the spot where love was found,
A treasure unearthed, forever profound.

Lost and found in moments rare,
The map we hold, beyond compare.
With ink of hope, we sketch our fate,
No matter the distance, we navigate.

Through seasons passed, we journey on,
Together, we write our timeless song.
For in this map, our souls entwine,
Forever bound, your heart in mine.

Seasons of Discovery

Spring awakens, blooms unfold,
Each petal whispers stories untold.
Fresh beginnings dance in the air,
Nature's canvas, colors flare.

Summer's warmth ignites our dreams,
Golden rays and sunlit beams.
Adventures call with joyful cheer,
Moments cherished, year after year.

Autumn paints with hues so bold,
Leaves cascade like dreams of gold.
Reflection deepens in twilight's glow,
A time to savor, a time to grow.

Winter wraps the earth in white,
A quiet pause, with stars alight.
In the stillness, we find our peace,
A gentle slowing, a sweet release.

Each season whispers, secrets to find,
In every change, we leave our blind.
Through cycles turning, we come to see,
Discovery lives in you and me.

Moments in Transition

In the pause between day and night,
We find the change, a subtle light.
Shadows stretch, horizons blend,
Every ending, a chance to mend.

Paths diverge, a choice to make,
With every turn, new paths to take.
The heart beats fast, uncertain yet strong,
In moments fleeting, we learn to belong.

Whispers echo, doubts arise,
Change can sting, but it also ties.
With open arms, we greet the new,
Embracing all that we pursue.

In every breath, we seek and find,
A shift is coming, a different kind.
As seasons shift, so do we grow,
In the dance of life, we learn to flow.

So here we stand, on bridges wide,
With courage born from deep inside.
Moments in transition lead the way,
To brighter tomorrows, day by day.

Ruins to Revelations

Amidst the stones, stories lie,
Whispers of time that drift and sigh.
Crumbled walls tell of old grace,
Echoing dreams of a lost place.

Once proud towers kiss the sky,
Unraveled dreams begin to die.
Nature reclaims what man has built,
In shadows dwell the threads of guilt.

Fragments scatter, lost in thought,
Lessons in ruins long forgot.
What was built has fallen low,
Yet in the dust, new seeds must grow.

Through the wreckage, hope is found,
From shattered dreams, new lives abound.
Each stone a chapter, each crack a line,
In the story of a world divine.

Signs of Our Voyage

Sails kissed the wind, hearts full of dreams,
Charted waters with whispered themes.
Each wave a challenge, each star a guide,
Navigating truths where shadows abide.

The compass points to the unknown,
In distant horizons, adventures have grown.
With every sunset, a tale unfolds,
As twilight cradles our hopes and holds.

Oceans speak in a language old,
Stories of voyages, brave and bold.
We weave our paths through serenity's call,
Knowing we rise, yet, sometimes we fall.

Each port a chapter, each anchor a pause,
Finding our rhythm, obeying the laws.
In every journey, there's beauty and strife,
Through all the chaos, we discover life.

Mosaic of Memories

Fragments of moments, colors collide,
A canvas of time where shadows abide.
Each piece a story, a lost memory,
Together they form our history.

Whispers of laughter mixed with tears,
Dances of joy through the passing years.
In the patchwork of days, we find our art,
Mapping the journeys that shape the heart.

Silhouettes linger in sunlit streams,
Echoes of hopes woven in dreams.
Life's gentle brush paints love and woe,
With every stroke, we learn and grow.

Through broken tiles, beauty gleams,
Life's imperfections are what it seems.
A mosaic crafted by hands sublime,
Telling our tale across the sands of time.

Harmony in Motion

Dancing leaves in a twilight breeze,
Nature's rhythm brings hearts at ease.
The river sings of tales untold,
In harmony's echo, memories unfold.

Footfalls in sync with the tempo of day,
Guided by whispers that lead the way.
In the symphony of stars, we play our part,
Each note a heartbeat, each pause a start.

The sun dips low, painting skies bright,
As shadows join in the waltz of night.
Life flows like music, a dance of grace,
Every moment embraced in its place.

Together we sway to the world's embrace,
Finding our rhythm, our sacred space.
In harmony's cradle, our spirits rise,
A melody woven beneath the skies.

Navigating Our Story

With maps in hand, we sail the seas,
Charting a course through shifting breeze.
Every star guides our heart's intent,
In this vast world, our love is lent.

Through storms that test our faith anew,
We find the path, just me and you.
Each moment shared, a treasure keeps,
In the journey's depth, our promise sleeps.

With compass true, we face each dawn,
In the light of hope, we carry on.
Our story unfolds like waves on shore,
Together stronger, forevermore.

From peaks of joy to valleys low,
In every twist, our spirits grow.
Together we write our timeless tale,
Navigating love, we'll never fail.

So here's to us, the dreamers bold,
In the book of life, our love's retold.
With every chapter, our hearts explore,
Navigating our story evermore.

Uncharted Love

In the quiet dusk, two hearts collide,
With whispered dreams that cannot hide.
We fill the spaces, our souls entwine,
In this uncharted love, so divine.

Through secret paths, we make our claim,
No maps to guide, no rules to tame.
Every glance a spark, a mystery,
In this wild dance, just you and me.

With every heartbeat, we forge ahead,
Unknown adventures, yet unafraid.
We wander freely, hand in hand,
In this vast world, we make our stand.

The compass spins, we lose our way,
But in the chaos, we choose to stay.
From mountain high to ocean deep,
In uncharted love, our dreams we keep.

So let the winds of fate decide,
We'll brave the storms, with love our guide.
Together, we write what fate can't see,
In this uncharted love, just you and me.

Echoes of Our Adventure

Beneath the stars, we took our flight,
Chasing dreams in the velvet night.
With laughter bold, we climbed so high,
Echoes of our adventure fill the sky.

Every step, a story spun,
In unison, our hearts have won.
Through winding paths and unseen bends,
Our love, a force, that never ends.

In whispered tales, we find our thrill,
With promise strong, we bend to will.
From valleys low to peaks so bright,
In echoes of our adventure, we ignite.

The world unfurls, a canvas wide,
With every brush, we dare to glide.
Together painted, our masterpiece,
In the echoes of love, we find our peace.

As shadows fade and dawn's light breaks,
We carry forth with every wake.
In the footprints left upon the shore,
Echoes of our adventure, forevermore.

Winding Roads to Home

Along the winding roads we tread,
Together strong, by love we're led.
Through twists and turns, we find our way,
With every mile, our hearts convey.

With whispers soft, we share our dreams,
In the dance of life, we find our themes.
The sun may set, but paths will bloom,
As we journey forth, we make a room.

In fleeting moments, laughter sings,
Through trials faced, our love takes wings.
With every challenge, side by side,
Winding roads to home, our hearts abide.

So take my hand, we'll face the night,
In shadows cast, we find our light.
With open hearts, we'll roam so free,
On winding roads, just you and me.

Through all the journeys yet to come,
In every beat, our hearts will drum.
For in this life, where love may bloom,
We'll find our way, we'll build our home.

Step by Step to Forever

With every heartbeat drawing near,
Promises whispered, loud and clear.
Through the shadows, hand in hand,
We walk together, understand.

Each step taken, faith in sight,
Lighting paths with love's pure light.
In the silence, vows replay,
Step by step, we find our way.

Time may fade, yet we will stay,
In the moments, come what may.
Building dreams that never cease,
Step by step, we find our peace.

Through the storms and sunny skies,
Our love grows strong, it never dies.
Set our sights on the unknown,
Together, we have always grown.

Forever is a journey, long,
In your arms, I know I belong.
With each footfall, hearts align,
Step by step, your hand in mine.

Unfolding Stories

Every page holds whispers sweet,
Tales of lives with trails to meet.
In the moonlight, secrets gleam,
Hearts entwined in a shared dream.

Seasons pass, but words remain,
Etched in laughter, love, and pain.
Every chapter, lessons learned,
In our hearts, the flames have burned.

Dancing through the days and nights,
Writing stories of our flights.
With each glance, a spark ignites,
Unfolding tales, our love's delights.

Ink and paper, timeless truths,
Chasing dreams from eager youths.
With each story, bonds grow tight,
Unfolding love, pure and bright.

In the silence, echoes call,
Whispers of the rise and fall.
Together still, we'll brave the storm,
Crafting stories, forever warm.

The Dance of Companionship

In the twilight, shadows sway,
Two souls twirling, night and day.
With each twinkle, steps align,
In this dance, your heart is mine.

Rhythms blend in soft embrace,
Life's sweet music fills the space.
Every turn, a silent vow,
Together dancing, here and now.

Through the laughter, through the tears,
We'll keep dancing through the years.
Let the world fade out of sight,
In your arms, the stars ignite.

Time may try to steal the day,
Yet our dance will find a way.
With every step, our love expands,
Two hearts waltzing, hand in hand.

In the silence, whispers grow,
Companionship, a gentle flow.
With each beat, forever near,
In this dance, I hold you dear.

Alongside the Stars

Underneath the vast expanse,
We lay dreaming in a trance.
Stars above, our wishes shared,
In their glow, we felt prepared.

Every twinkle tells a tale,
Of our journey, love's own trail.
As the night drapes soft and deep,
In this moment, dreams we'll keep.

Guided by the silver light,
We explore the endless night.
Together, we'll chase the beams,
Finding worlds within our dreams.

Galaxies will call our name,
In their wonders, stoke the flame.
Together, we will wait and soar,
Alongside stars, forevermore.

In the quiet, hearts align,
Reaching out, your hand in mine.
With the cosmos as our guide,
Alongside stars, we shall abide.

Bridges of Understanding

Across the river, we meet in grace,
With open hearts, no time to waste.
Each word a step, each smile a sign,
Building bridges, yours and mine.

In silence, we share what cannot be said,
Unveiling truths, where fears once tread.
With patience, we learn to mend the rift,
Together we rise, together we lift.

Through storms and shadows, we hold on tight,
Finding our way, igniting the light.
In every challenge, a lesson we find,
Bridges of hope, with love intertwined.

So let us walk on this path we've forged,
With every connection, our spirits enlarged.
Hand in hand, as we traverse the land,
Embracing all that's truly grand.

Travel Beyond the Horizon

The sun dips low, the sky ignites,
With whispers of dreams, our hearts take flight.
Beyond the horizon, we chase the day,
In every sunset, we find our way.

Mountains await, their peaks so high,
With courage amassed, together we fly.
In valleys of green, our laughter rings,
Every adventure, new joy it brings.

Through cities bright and oceans vast,
We gather memories, shadows cast.
Each footprint echoes the paths we've taken,
With every journey, new bonds awaken.

When clouds obscure the stars above,
We dance in the rain, wrapped in love.
For travel's more than places we see,
It's moments shared, just you and me.

The Art of Us

In colors of laughter, our canvas unfolds,
Brushstrokes of love in stories retold.
With every moment, a masterpiece grows,
In the art of us, pure beauty flows.

We paint our dreams in shades of bold,
Together we bloom, our hearts turned gold.
With every challenge, our palette expands,
Creating the magic that life demands.

In whispers of trust, we find our muse,
With colors collided, we choose to fuse.
Each heartbeat echoes a rhythm divine,
Crafting the art that forever will shine.

So let's dance to the tune of our creation,
In the gallery of life, pure celebration.
With love as our guide, we'll forever be,
The art of us, just you and me.

Strokes of Shared Moments

Time paints a canvas with strokes of laughter,
Each moment we cherish, a life we capture.
In shadows and light, our stories align,
Strokes of shared moments, forever entwined.

We gather the echoes of days long past,
Moments we share, each one meant to last.
With smiles that sparkle and tears that flow,
Through strokes of our friendship, together we grow.

In fleeting time, memories stay bright,
Captured in frames of warmth and light.
Each heartbeat remembered, a gift that we share,
Strokes of connection, beyond compare.

So let us gather these moments so dear,
In the art of living, let's draw them near.
With colors of passion, our lives will blend,
In strokes of shared moments, love knows no end.

Eternal Echoes of Together

In twilight's glow, we find our way,
Hand in hand, through night and day.
Whispers linger in the air,
Promises made, beyond compare.

As stars align, our spirits dance,
In every moment, there's a chance.
Time stands still, yet flows like streams,
Together, we weave our dreams.

In laughter shared, in silence deep,
Memories cherished, secrets to keep.
Through storms we stand, unbroken, bold,
Eternal echoes, tales retold.

With every sigh, love's gentle breeze,
Carving paths among the trees.
In shadows cast, we find our light,
Eternal echoes of our flight.

When morning breaks, and dawns arise,
We'll chase the sun across the skies.
In every heartbeat, every tether,
Together, forever, through any weather.

Carved in Memory

In ancient wood, our names are stilled,
Time etches love, our lives fulfilled.
Each ring a story, whispered low,
In every grain, the past will flow.

Beneath the sky, our dreams took seed,
In laughter's sigh, in whispered need.
Moments captured, forever held,
In memory's light, our hearts compelled.

Through seasons change, we stand our ground,
In every silence, love is found.
The tapestry of days entwined,
In threads of gold, the past defined.

As sunsets fade, and stars align,
We carve our tales, our fates entwined.
In echoes soft, our spirits soar,
Carved in memory, forevermore.

Narratives of Our Hearts

In whispered tones, our stories rise,
Ink of the soul, beneath the skies.
Each heartbeat tells a tale anew,
Narratives woven, me and you.

Through trials faced and joys embraced,
In every moment, love is laced.
Pages turning with every breath,
Chronicling life's dance with death.

In laughter shared, in shadows cast,
The present held, the future vast.
Within each glance, the worlds we bring,
Narratives of hearts, in love we sing.

With every sigh, and every tear,
The chapters bloom, as paths appear.
In memories penned, we gain our art,
Tales unfolding from the heart.

Clouds of Possibility

Upon the horizon, dreams take flight,
Clouds of possibility, pure and bright.
In every shade, a chance to soar,
An open sky, inviting more.

With every whisper of the wind,
New adventures waiting to begin.
In shadows cast by fleeting rays,
The heart ignites in hopeful blaze.

Through stormy weather, through rain's embrace,
We look beyond, find our place.
In every challenge, a lesson learned,
Clouds of possibility brightly turned.

In laughter shared, in nights unbound,
We chase the stars, new dreams we've found.
With every step, we break the mold,
Towards horizons yet untold.

So let us dance on skies of blue,
With open hearts, and spirits true.
In every cloud, a story spins,
Possibilities soar where hope begins.

Tides of Together

In the moon's soft glow, waves collide,
Hearts entwined, we turn the tide.
With every crest, love's gentle call,
Together we rise, together we fall.

Footprints in sand, we leave behind,
Whispers of love, effortlessly aligned.
As seashells gather, dreams unfold,
In the tides of together, our story told.

Beneath the stars, a secret shared,
Through storms and calms, we have dared.
With each swell, our bond's reinforced,
In the currents of life, we're lovingly sourced.

Through dusk and dawn, our spirits roam,
In the dance of waves, we find our home.
The horizon beckons, vast and wide,
In the tides of together, ever our guide.

We navigate life's endless sea,
For in each other, we truly see.
With every heartbeat, steadfast and true,
In the tides of together, it's me and you.

The Dance of Destinies

In shadows cast by fateful strands,
We twirl beneath time's gentle hands.
Each step a choice, each turn a chance,
Together we leap in destiny's dance.

The universe swirls, entwined with fate,
Unraveling dreams that we create.
With every whisper, our paths aligned,
In this ballroom of life, our souls combined.

Through trials faced and triumphs shared,
A tapestry woven, moments bared.
As stars align in cosmic glee,
In the dance of destinies, just you and me.

With every heartbeat, rhythms arise,
Echoing love beneath boundless skies.
In the stillness, we find our grace,
In the dance of destinies, we embrace.

As the music fades and shadows play,
We hold on tight, come what may.
For in this waltz, forever we'll sway,
In the dance of destinies, night turns to day.

Horizons of Belonging

Beneath the sun's warm, golden glare,
We search for places that truly care.
In fields of hope, we run and sing,
In the horizons of belonging, we find our wings.

Mountains rise and valleys fall,
With every journey, we heed the call.
In laughter shared and moments bright,
Horizons beckon, guiding our flight.

Together we paint, with colors bold,
Stories of dreams, waiting to unfold.
With every sunset, our hearts will soar,
In the horizons of belonging, we seek for more.

Through whispered winds and gentle sighs,
In every glance, our love complies.
In the embrace of the earth so strong,
In the horizons of belonging, we belong.

This path we're on, forever we tread,
Hand in hand, with hopes widespread.
Through every trial, our spirits long,
In the horizons of belonging, we grow strong.

Threads of Fate

In the loom of time, threads intertwine,
Each moment stitched, a design divine.
With hands united, we weave our tale,
In the threads of fate, we shall prevail.

Seasons change and colors shift,
Life's tapestry is our precious gift.
Through joy and sorrow, laughter and strife,
In the threads of fate, we shape our life.

A needle's eye, where dreams pass through,
In every stitch, a promise true.
With every knot, our love is laid,
In the threads of fate, never afraid.

As patterns form, a picture bright,
Together we journey, hearts alight.
In this fabric of life, bold and great,
We find our peace in the threads of fate.

Through tangled paths and winding ways,
Our spirits shine in myriad ways.
With every heartbeat, our paths create,
In the threads of fate, we celebrate.

Stepping Stones and Heartbeats

In the quiet dusk of evening light,
We tread softly, heartbeats in tune,
Every step a whispered secret,
Carved in shadows of the moon.

Beyond the gravel, past the streams,
Stepping stones lead us on and on,
With each leap our courage gleams,
Together we chase the dawn.

Moments flutter like autumn leaves,
Caught in the arms of gentle air,
We share our dreams, our quiet weaves,
In the fabric of time we dare.

Footprints whisper on the ground,
Echoes of laughter sweetly flow,
In this journey, love profound,
We find our way, we learn to grow.

Every heartbeat, every sigh,
Tells a story of here and now,
Together we reach for the sky,
With stepping stones, we learn to vow.

Footsteps into Tomorrow

As sunlight breaks through morning's haze,
We gather strength from what is true,
Each footprint etched in golden rays,
Is a promise made anew.

Though paths may twist, though shadows loom,
We walk with faith, hand in hand,
Each heartbeat fuels the brightened bloom,
In a world so vast and grand.

Tomorrow's dreams are seeds we sow,
With every step, our roots grow deep,
Through storms and trials, we must go,
With love, our hearts forever keep.

Together we face the rising tide,
In the dance of fate and chance,
With open arms, we won't divide,
For in unity lies our stance.

Time may bend, but we stay strong,
Footsteps echo, a timeless song,
In this journey, where we belong,
We step towards where dreams prolong.

Paths of Togetherness

On winding roads where echoes meet,
We carve our names in nature's script,
Side by side with hungry feet,
In every moment, love's equipped.

Through forests deep and valleys wide,
Together we navigate the trails,
With laughter shared, in joy, we bide,
Creating stories that never pale.

Each step a thread in the fabric spun,
Of friendship, trust, and sweet embrace,
With light that dances, shadows run,
As we explore this sacred space.

Hand in hand we rise and fall,
In the rhythm of the open air,
Every stumble, every call,
Brings us closer, a bond we share.

Through tangled paths, our spirits soar,
With every heartbeat, we explore,
In the tapestry of forevermore,
Together we find the open door.

Threads of Connection

In the web of life, we find our way,
Each thread we weave, a story told,
With love and laughter, come what may,
Our spirits warm against the cold.

Through tangled fears and hopes so bright,
We stitch our dreams with care and grace,
In every moment, hearts ignite,
Creating bonds no time can erase.

Together we stand, a vibrant quilt,
Each piece a memory, rich and bold,
In the tapestry of joy we've built,
Every color a tale of gold.

With hands entwined, we face the day,
Aware of threads that bind us tight,
In connection, light shall sway,
Guiding us through the darkest night.

As seasons change and shadows blend,
We'll cherish the ties that remain,
For in these threads, we find the blend,
Of love eternal, free from pain.

Beneath the Same Moon

Under the glow of soft silver light,
Whispers of dreams dance in the night.
Hearts are connected, though miles apart,
The same moon caresses each beating heart.

Stars twinkle brightly, painting our skies,
In silence, we share our deepest sighs.
Wishes float freely on gentle breeze,
Together, yet lost in memories' ease.

Clouds may obscure our paths for a while,
But faith lights our way with each hopeful smile.
In shadows we find the strength to endure,
Beneath the same moon, our love feels pure.

Time does not bind us, nor distance define,
Threads of affection eternally intertwine.
With every heartbeat, the world feels right,
Connected forever beneath stars so bright.

So here's to the love that we nurture and grow,
Under the moonlight, with hearts all aglow.
Together we thrive, even when far away,
Beneath the same moon, we'll find our way.

Signposts of Affection

On winding roads where our laughter rings,
Signposts of love, oh, what joy it brings!
Each step together, a story unfolds,
Tales of our hearts, in whispers retold.

Every glance shared, a promise we make,
In the dance of the night, no dream is at stake.
Through trials and triumphs, our bond will prevail,
With love as our compass, we shall not fail.

Moments like jewels, each one we embrace,
In the map of our lives, it's love we trace.
Through storms and sunshine, we wander with grace,
Signposts of affection guide us through space.

Together we travel, no distance too far,
Held by the light of our own guiding star.
With laughter and warmth, our spirits will soar,
Each signpost a memory, we cherish the more.

So here's to our journey, whatever the track,
With love as our guide, there's no turning back.
With hearts intertwined, we're destined to roam,
Signposts of affection lead us back home.

Journeying Beyond

Each step we take marks the path we roam,
Journeying beyond, together we call home.
The world is vast, but our hearts are near,
In every adventure, I hold you dear.

Mountains and valleys, we traverse with care,
Holding each other in moments we share.
With courage and faith, we traverse unknown,
In love's gentle light, we are never alone.

Through rivers and forests, across oceans wide,
With you by my side, I feel joy and pride.
Every challenge faced, a testament true,
Journeying beyond, where dreams all come through.

With stars as our guides, we'll write our own tale,
Sailing through skies, on love's steady sail.
No map can define what our hearts have found,
In journeying beyond, our souls are unbound.

So let's chase horizons, embrace what's in store,
With love leading us, we'll always want more.
An odyssey tender, forever we'll blend,
Journeying beyond, where love has no end.

The Mapmakers of Love

With ink and a dream, we sketch out our fate,
The mapmakers of love, we navigate late.
Each journey we take is a treasure to find,
In the folds of our hearts, our stories entwined.

Through valleys of laughter and mountains of tears,
We chart out the moments that conquer our fears.
With every curve drawn, a memory lives,
In the landscape of love, our hearts freely give.

From sketches to dreams, from whispers to sighs,
We trace our connection beneath endless skies.
Each line that we draw forms a path in the night,
The mapmakers of love, our future shines bright.

With every direction, we choose to explore,
In love's endless journey, we seek evermore.
Together we venture, through lands yet unknown,
The mapmakers of love, forever have grown.

So here's to the journeys that lie on the way,
With every new map, our hearts will display.
In the art of our love, we'll always be true,
The mapmakers of love, just me and you.

Skylines of Together

In twilight's grace, we stand as one,
Horizons stretch where day is done.
With dreams like stars, our hopes ignite,
We paint the skies in colors bright.

The city hums, a living song,
Each heartbeat echoes, where we belong.
Hand in hand, through night we roam,
In every skyline, we've found our home.

The laughter dances in the breeze,
Whispers carried by the trees.
Amidst the lights, our spirits soar,
Together always, forever more.

With every glance, a promise shared,
In every moment, love declared.
Through bustling streets, our paths align,
Two souls entwined, a fate divine.

As dawn awakens, colors blend,
Our journey melds, no need to pretend.
In skylines vast, we've made our mark,
Together we shine, lighting the dark.

Footprints on Shared Sand

Beneath the sun, we walk as one,
The waves embrace, the day begun.
With every step, our laughter flows,
In sandy trails, our love still grows.

The ocean whispers, tales so sweet,
In footprints left, our hearts compete.
An endless dance, the tide will sway,
Yet in this sand, we choose to stay.

As seagulls call, we gaze ahead,
In dreams of gold, our hopes are fed.
With every grain, a memory made,
In life's vast sea, our bond won't fade.

The sunset paints the sky aglow,
With hues of love, the tides we know.
We walk together, side by side,
In shared footprints, our hearts abide.

As night descends, the stars will shine,
In soft moonlight, our lives entwine.
With every wave, a promise stands,
Forever etched in shared sands.

Chronicles of Our Hearts

In whispered words, our stories weave,
A tapestry where dreams believe.
With every page, our souls entwine,
In chronicles of love, we shine.

The ink that flows, a deep embrace,
Each moment captured, a sacred space.
Through trials faced and journeys shared,
In every chapter, love declared.

With laughter written in the lines,
And tears that blend like vintage wines.
We craft our tales with heart and grace,
In every passage, we find our place.

The chapters turn, yet still we write,
In every dawn, a new delight.
With every glance, a spark ignites,
In chronicles of love, we unite.

As time moves on, our story grows,
In every heartbeat, our love bestows.
In pages worn, our legacy stays,
In chronicles of hearts, love lays.

Lanterns in the Night

In shadows deep, where silence reigns,
We find our light, where hope remains.
With lanterns bright, our spirits shine,
In darkest hours, our hearts align.

The stars above, they guide our way,
In whispered dreams, we choose to stay.
With every flicker, our hopes take flight,
A dance of love beneath the night.

Through winding paths, our lanterns glow,
With every step, new seeds we sow.
In gentle breezes, our wishes sail,
Together bound in love's rich trail.

The moonlit waves, a serenade,
In every moment, love is made.
We chase the dawn, but night is ours,
In lanterns lit, we heal our scars.

So let us wander, hand in hand,
With lanterns bright, we'll take a stand.
In whispers soft, our dreams ignite,
Together forever, lanterns in the night.

The Light We Share

In shadows deep, we find our glow,
A spark ignites, the warmth will flow.
Together we rise, hearts intertwined,
With every laugh, our souls aligned.

Through darkest nights, we face the fears,
In whispered words, we dry the tears.
A beacon bright, our hopes collide,
In unity's embrace, we bide.

The path ahead, with light we tread,
With every step, our spirit led.
Shining bright, we'll never part,
For love's the light that guides the heart.

Castles Built in Dreams

In fields of gold, our visions grow,
With every wish, the flowers sow.
We craft our walls from hopes and schemes,
A refuge found in softer themes.

As starlit skies embrace the night,
Each dream we weave, a future bright.
In whispered thoughts, our castles rise,
A kingdom born from painted skies.

With laughter sweet, we dance and play,
In regal halls, we find our way.
Together strong, we'll break the seams,
In endless joy, our hearts as beams.

Steps of Solid Ground

Each step we take, a presence known,
With every stride, our strength has grown.
Through trials faced, we learn to stand,
In steady hearts, we find the land.

The rhythm beats, a steady thrum,
In faith we walk, to what's become.
With open arms, the world we greet,
In every path, our souls repeat.

Through winding trails, we'll carve our fate,
In unity, we elevate.
With steady gaze, we chase the dawn,
Together here, we all belong.

Flames of Unity

In roaring fires, our spirits blend,
With every flame, our hearts ascend.
Together strong, we rise as one,
In unity, our battles won.

As flickers dance and shadows sway,
Our voices joined, they light the way.
A bond unbroken, forged in heat,
In harmony, our hearts will meet.

With passion bright, we stand so tall,
In every spark, we heed the call.
As flames entwine, we greet the night,
For in this fire, we're born to fight.

Reflections on the Way

Beneath the sky so wide,
I ponder paths I've tread.
Each step, a silent guide,
where dreams and memories spread.

In echoes of the past,
I find a whispered truth.
The shadows that were cast
now glow with fading youth.

The stars above me gleam,
like wishes left behind.
They pull me into dreams,
as time's soft fingers bind.

Reflections dance on streams,
where moments ebb and flow.
Each ripple speaks in themes
of journeys one must know.

The road is winding still,
with stories to unfold.
A heart that bends to will
finds peace in paths of old.

Steps Towards Together

With every step we take,
our hands entwined as one.
The world before us breaks
into a new day's sun.

The laughter that we share,
along this winding trail,
colors the empty air,
like ships with billowed sail.

In moments intertwined,
our hopes and fears combine.
The path is well-defined,
yet full of love's design.

We wander with a dream,
braving the ups and downs.
Together, we redeem
the scattered shades of frowns.

With every chosen turn,
a bond begins to grow.
In unity, we learn
the strength of hearts aglow.

Beyond the Crossroads

They stand like ancient signs,
these choices laid in stone.
With heart and mind that binds,
we carve our way alone.

Each road a different tale,
and paths both dark and bright.
Through storms we will not fail,
as stars will guide our sight.

The whispers of the past,
a chorus in the night.
They teach us to hold fast,
embracing wrong and right.

We gather all the strength,
and tread to find our fate.
Collecting dreams at length,
we chase what makes us great.

Beyond the crossroads stand,
a future yet unknown.
With courage close at hand,
we journey forth alone.

Whispers Along the Path

Along the winding way,
a gentle breeze does sigh.
It carries hopes that stay,
and dreams that choose to fly.

The rustle of the leaves,
a sonnet sung by trees.
In nature, the heart weaves
a tapestry of peace.

In shadows that embrace,
there's solace to be found.
Each footfall, a soft grace,
in silence wraps around.

Beneath the arching boughs,
I feel the past arise.
A symphony of vows
that echoes in the skies.

As sun creeps through the shade,
it paints the path anew.
In whispers, we parade
a journey sweet and true.

Reflections on Our Path

We walk upon a winding road,
With dreams and hopes in heavy loads.
The past behind, a tale to tell,
In every step, we rise and fell.

Through shadows deep, we find our light,
A compass guiding, shining bright.
The choices made, both right and wrong,
They shape our hearts, they make us strong.

With every turn, a lesson learned,
A flame of wisdom gently burned.
Together we seek, together we strive,
In unity, we feel alive.

The future calls, its voice a song,
In every heartbeat, we belong.
So let us walk, hand in hand,
On this path, so vast and grand.

In twilight's glow, we find our way,
Through night and dawn, we greet the day.
Each memory crafted, a precious art,
Reflections echoing in the heart.

Skylines of Dreams

Beneath the stars, our hopes take flight,
In the skyline bright, they dance at night.
Each dream a spark, a guiding star,
Illuminating paths both near and far.

We build our towers, reaching high,
With every brick, we touch the sky.
In whispered winds, our voices soar,
Echoes of dreams, forevermore.

The colors blend, a vibrant hue,
In every sunset, a promise true.
Boundless visions, hearts aligned,
In the skyline of dreams, peace we find.

Through storms we weather, we remain bold,
In unity, our stories told.
Each setback shapes what we can be,
In the canvas of life, we are free.

Together we rise, together we gleam,
In the embrace of a shimmering dream.
Every heartbeat, a note of grace,
In the skyline of our shared space.

The Canvas We Paint

With vivid strokes, our lives unfold,
A canvas blank, stories untold.
Colors mingle, bright and bold,
In the masterpiece, our truths behold.

Each moment captured, a fleeting glance,
In every hue, a silent dance.
The brush of time, it moves so fast,
Yet memories linger, meant to last.

We blend our dreams with shades of pain,
In every drop, a lesson gained.
A tapestry woven, rich and deep,
In the canvas of life, secrets we keep.

Through storms and sunshine, we create,
Each line and curve, a twist of fate.
From chaos born, we find our way,
In art, we strive, we hope, we play.

With every heartbeat, the colors change,
In the gallery of life, we rearrange.
Together we paint, side by side,
In the canvas of dreams, we'll abide.

Unveiling the Unknown

In shadows deep, we seek the light,
Unveiling mysteries hidden from sight.
With every step, we pierce the veil,
Unlocking secrets where dreams prevail.

The whispers of fate call us near,
Each heartbeat echoing, crystal clear.
Through the fog, we tread with care,
In quest for truth, our hearts laid bare.

With open minds, we chase the dawn,
Embracing challenges, we're reborn.
The unknown beckons, wild and free,
In its embrace, we find the key.

In all the chaos, beauty shines,
Through tangled paths, a force divine.
As horizons shift, we come to know,
In the dance of life, we all can grow.

So let us wander, hand in hand,
In the realm of dreams, we make our stand.
For in unveiling the unknown's worth,
We find our place, our true rebirth.

Across the Timeless Sea

Waves whisper tales of old,
Hearts set sail, brave and bold.
Beneath the stars, we drift and dream,
Guided by the moon's soft beam.

Every tide brings new desires,
A dance of joy, like ancient choirs.
Shores of time, where memories play,
We voyage forth, come what may.

In the horizon's fading light,
Seagulls call, taking flight.
Across the sea, our souls unite,
Together, we face the night.

The ocean's song, a lullaby,
As whispers fade, we learn to fly.
Each wave a promise, strong and true,
In every journey, I find you.

Together, we'll chart unknown lands,
Hand in hand, amidst shifting sands.
With every sunset, a story told,
Across the sea, our love unfolds.

Soulprints on the Earth

In the forest, leaves will sigh,
Tracing paths where spirits fly.
Every step marks a gentle trace,
Nature holds us in its embrace.

Footprints linger, soft and light,
Whispers echo in the night.
Roots entwine as legends grow,
In the earth, our stories flow.

Clouds above weave tales of yore,
In each storm, we love once more.
Sunset paints the sky with grace,
Memories etched in nature's face.

Mountains rise to greet our dreams,
Rivers dance with silver beams.
Every heart bears a silent worth,
Together, we imprint the earth.

In fields of gold, we lay our claim,
In the soil, we stake our name.
Soulprints left in sacred ground,
In love and light, we are bound.

Moments That Bind

In laughter shared, the world feels bright,
In quiet glances, hearts take flight.
Each fleeting second, a golden thread,
Weave it gently, where love is led.

Through trials faced, and joys we seek,
In soft-spoken words, no need to speak.
Every heartbeat draws us near,
In every moment, you hold me dear.

Time loses shape, when we align,
In sacred space, our lives entwine.
Memories linger, like stars that shine,
In these moments, our souls combine.

Tangled paths, we wander wide,
With open arms, we turn the tide.
In simple gestures, profound grace,
Every moment finds its place.

Together we build our dreamlike frame,
Every whisper calls your name.
In each heartbeat, our spirits find,
The sweetest song of moments kind.

The Tapestry of Together

Threads of laughter, colors bright,
Weaving memories in the light.
Each strand carries a tale of old,
In our tapestry, love is bold.

Fingers entwined, we create a design,
Every twist and turn, a sacred sign.
In shadows cast, and sunlight's gleam,
Together we stitch, a living dream.

Fabric of life, rich and warm,
In storms we shelter, our hearts transform.
Every pattern tells of our strife,
In every stitch, the art of life.

Through trials faced, and joys we share,
In the weave of hope, we show we care.
With every thread, our story grows,
A masterpiece only time knows.

Together we craft, with love and grace,
In this tapestry, we find our place.
A legacy of hearts combined,
In this world, forever intertwined.

Hearts in Confluence

In the quiet of our night,
Stars align, hearts take flight.
Two souls dance in the glow,
A river of love starts to flow.

Winds whisper sweet refrain,
Embracing joys, easing pain.
Together we brave the storm,
In your arms, my heart is warm.

Branches weave, shadows play,
In this moment, we shall stay.
Trust builds like a sturdy bridge,
On this path, love takes the ridge.

With every laugh and sigh,
In the depths, our spirits fly.
Harmony sings a tune,
Two hearts beneath the moon.

Timeless bonds, forever found,
In each heartbeat, love resounds.
Indelible paths we trace,
In your gaze, a secret place.

The Space Between Us

In the silence, a soft sigh,
Where unspoken words lie.
Echoes linger, shadows stretch,
Searching for what we can't fetch.

Dreams drift on whispered winds,
Choosing paths that love begins.
In this void, feelings grow,
Lessons only time can show.

Fingers brush, electric spark,
Illuminating the dark.
Every heartbeat draws us near,
Yet the distance feels so clear.

Time can bend, but not erase,
All the memories we embrace.
In the space where hopes reside,
Love's own rhythm, our guide.

Let's bridge this gap with care,
Finding strength in what we share.
With each glance, a promise made,
Together, we won't fade.

Echoes of Tomorrow

Whispers dance on the breeze,
Carrying dreams with such ease.
Footprints left in golden sand,
Memories vast, beautifully planned.

Hope blooms in the morning light,
Chasing shadows of the night.
Every promise, etched in time,
With each heartbeat, a new rhyme.

In the laughter, stories unfold,
Futures bright, waiting to be told.
Together we paint the skies,
Colors rich, no goodbyes.

Every moment sparks a flame,
In this journey, find our name.
Chasing echoes far and wide,
In love's embrace, we abide.

As the dusk begins to fall,
We'll embrace it, standing tall.
In the twilight, we'll soar high,
With echoes that never die.

Crossroads of Connection

At dusk where paths entwine,
A moment timeless and divine.
Eyes meet, a silent call,
In this space, we find our all.

Winding roads, a shared embrace,
In kindness, we find our place.
Hands entwined, worlds collide,
With hope and love as our guide.

Choices made bring hearts anew,
In your light, I see what's true.
Every step, a dance we share,
In this journey, we're laid bare.

Words unspoken, yet so clear,
In your presence, there's no fear.
Through the trials, we shall stand,
Side by side, hand in hand.

As dawn breaks, we'll find our way,
With every heartbeat, come what may.
In the crossroads, love will thrive,
Together, always, we'll arrive.

Whispers of Our Odyssey

In the quiet night we sail,
Stars above, a guiding trail.
Waves of time, they softly hum,
Whispers call where dreams come from.

Through the mist, we seek our way,
Echoes of the past at play.
Every heartbeat, every sigh,
Marks the course as we float by.

Beneath the moon, our secrets shared,
In this journey, we are paired.
Hand in hand, we brave the sea,
Bound together, you and me.

Voices blend in harmony,
As we chart our destiny.
With each breath, a new refrain,
Love's adventure, joy, and pain.

Towards horizons yet unknown,
In this voyage, we've both grown.
Whispers of our odyssey,
Forever etched in memory.

Tides of Connection

Rising sun and rolling tide,
In this place, our hearts collide.
Waves that pull and waves that push,
In this dance, we find our hush.

Moments shared beneath the stars,
Mapping dreams, we heal our scars.
Every heartbeat swells the sea,
Tides of love, you and me.

Laughter mingles with the breeze,
Whispers carried through the trees.
Every sunset paints our skies,
In your gaze, my spirit flies.

Through the storms, we stand as one,
Challenges met, battles won.
Connection deep as ocean's floor,
Together, we will rise and soar.

In the quiet, we will find,
Tides of love, forever kind.
Hand in hand, we face the day,
In this journey, come what may.

Threads of Heartbeat

In the tapestry of time,
Every thread, a perfect rhyme.
Stitched together, me and you,
A dance of colors, bright and true.

Heartbeat echoing through space,
In your presence, I find grace.
Woven tightly, hearts align,
In this fabric, love will shine.

Moments captured, joys unfold,
With each story, we are bold.
Threads of laughter, tears, and dreams,
In this weaving, hope redeems.

Through the seasons, we will grow,
Embracing all, high and low.
Every challenge, every cheer,
Threads of heartbeat, always near.

As we journey, side by side,
In this quilt, we take our pride.
Woven patterns, rich and deep,
In our hearts, these memories keep.

Through Fields of Destiny

In gentle breezes, dreams take flight,
Through fields where shadows kiss the light.
Every step, a chance to see,
Paths unwritten, you and me.

Golden flowers, bright and fair,
Whispers of fate dance in the air.
With each moment, we will grow,
Through fields where the wild winds blow.

Hand in hand, we walk along,
Nature's heartbeat, soft and strong.
Every meadow holds a tale,
In this journey, we prevail.

As the sun dips low and red,
In this beauty, fears we'll shed.
Fields of destiny, vast and wide,
Every dream, where hopes reside.

Through the night, we share our fears,
Embracing joy, dissolving tears.
In these fields, our hearts will soar,
Together, always longing for more.

Embracing the Distance

In twilight's glow, we part ways,
Yet in silence, our hearts stay.
With every mile, love's thread we weave,
In dreams, our souls believe.

The stars above, a guide so bright,
Remind us of our shared light.
Though time may stretch, our bond won't fray,
In whispers, we find our way.

Across the fields, where shadows play,
Your laughter echoes, night or day.
In every breeze, I sense your grace,
Together still, though in different space.

The world spins on, yet we remain,
Cradled close, in joy and pain.
Each heartbeat syncs, a distant pulse,
In this love, we are the result.

Embrace the distance, trust the touch,
For a bond like ours means so much.
In the spaces between, our spirits soar,
A journey together, forevermore.

Heartbeats in Harmony

Two souls merge, a gentle dance,
In rhythm, we find our chance.
With every beat, our hearts collide,
In this song, we shall abide.

Soft whispers echo, secrets shared,
In the silence, love declared.
With every sigh, we draw so near,
In every glance, we hold what's dear.

Like waves that crash upon the shore,
Our melodies forever roar.
A symphony born from tender trust,
In unity, we rise, we must.

Let time unfold, and dreams take flight,
In arms embracing, pure delight.
With every pulse, our spirits climb,
In the heartbeat, love's true rhyme.

Together we face the world unknown,
In harmony, we have grown.
Through every storm, through every fight,
Our heartbeats echo, pure and bright.

Maps of Us

With ink and dreams, we trace the line,
Of moments shared, both yours and mine.
Each laughter marks a path we've trod,
A journey mapped, in love's facade.

Through forests deep, and mountains high,
Our story unfolds beneath the sky.
Every map reveals our fate,
In the land of love, we navigate.

The compass spins, yet holds its ground,
In every heartbeat, truth is found.
Guided by stars, we chase the night,
Our hearts aligned, a guiding light.

With every turn, new fears we'll face,
But together, we'll find our place.
Through rivers wide and valleys low,
In the thread of time, our love will flow.

So hold my hand, as we embark,
On this map where love leaves a mark.
With every step, we journey true,
In the maps of us, I choose you.

Beneath the Shared Sky

In the quiet night, our wishes soar,
Two hearts united, forevermore.
Beneath the stars, we find our place,
In the vast expanse, we share a space.

The moonlight bathes our dreams in glow,
With whispered hopes, together we grow.
Each twinkle tells a tale untold,
Of love that burns, fierce and bold.

Through storms that rage and winds that wail,
Together we stand, we will not fail.
In the tapestry of night we weave,
A story of us, in fate we believe.

As dawn approaches, colors ignite,
Our hearts entwined in morning light.
With every daybreak, our love is reborn,
In the shared sky, new dreams are worn.

So hold this moment, close and dear,
In every heartbeat, you are near.
Beneath the vast and endless sky,
In love's embrace, we learn to fly.

The Call of Our Spirits

In the quiet of the night's embrace,
Whispers linger, a soft trace.
Hearts awaken before the dawn,
Echoes of love, forever drawn.

Voices rise on a gentle breeze,
Carrying dreams through ancient trees.
Together we stand, unbroken, bold,
In unity, our stories told.

From the shadows, our spirits soar,
Guided by stars to distant shores.
In every heartbeat, we find a way,
To chase the light of a brand new day.

Threads of hope weave through the night,
Binding our dreams, a shimmering light.
In the tapestry of longing deep,
We find the promises we keep.

As dawn approaches, fears will fade,
In the warmth, our bonds are made.
The call of our spirits, a timeless song,
Together we rise, where we belong.

Beneath the Canopy of Us

Beneath the leaves, a world unfolds,
Whispers of stories yet untold.
With laughter bright, we share our dreams,
In the sun's embrace, life gently gleams.

The rustling branches around us sway,
In harmony, we find our way.
With every step, the earth bears witness,
To our bond, a sacred sweetness.

As sunlight filters through the trees,
We breathe in the joy, the perfect ease.
In shadows cast, our hearts align,
A garden of love where we entwine.

The breeze carries tales of the past,
Yet in this moment, we hold fast.
Each shared glance, a silent vow,
To cherish the now, our spirits bow.

Together we dance in playful delight,
Beneath the canopy, everything feels right.
With every heartbeat, we feel the rush,
In the sanctuary of our trust.

Journeys of Kindred Souls

In journeys traveled, we find our way,
Through twists and turns, come what may.
With kindred spirits by our side,
In every step, love's gentle guide.

Across vast seas and mountain highs,
Together we chase the endless skies.
In laughter shared, our burdens lift,
A precious bond, our greatest gift.

With open hearts, we wander free,
Through valleys wide, by the old oak tree.
In silence shared, our souls connect,
With every glance, a deep respect.

The night unfolds, stars shining bright,
In the glow of friendship, we take flight.
With dreams as oars, we navigate,
Each moment cherished, we celebrate.

From sunrise gold to twilight hues,
Through every challenge, love imbues.
In journeys bold, we find our goal,
Forever entwined, two kindred souls.

The Fabric of Togetherness

In threads of gold, we weave our fate,
A tapestry rich, we cultivate.
Every color tells a tale,
Of joys and trials that never pale.

With every stitch, our hearts align,
In fabric strong, love's design.
Through laughter bright and sorrow's grace,
Together we find our sacred space.

The patterns shift, but never stray,
In unity, we find our way.
In moments shared, we stand as one,
Under the warmth of the setting sun.

From dawn's first light to evening's glow,
In the warmth of togetherness, we grow.
Every bind, a bond we make,
In the fabric of love, our spirits awake.

With gentle hands, we hold what's dear,
In every memory, we draw near.
A woven heart, forever drawn,
In the fabric of togetherness, we've won.

Milestones of the Heart

In whispers soft, we mark our days,
With laughter shared along the ways.
Each moment cherished, bound so tight,
A tapestry woven in golden light.

The journey long, yet time stands still,
As memories form, we learn and fill.
Each milestone reached, a story told,
A treasure kept, more worth than gold.

Through trials faced, we rise anew,
With every step, our spirits grew.
Together strong, as seasons change,
Our hearts align, though lives rearrange.

We hold the past, but gaze ahead,
In love's embrace, no words unsaid.
With every heartbeat, we draw the lines,
In this canvas of life, our love entwines.

So let us journey, hand in hand,
Through every shadow, across this land.
For every milestone that we meet,
Is but a step, a love complete.

Serendipitous Encounters

A fleeting glance in crowded halls,
Two strangers meet, as fate recalls.
A twist of chance, a spark ignites,
In endless wonder, joy unites.

Unplanned adventures, paths collide,
Unspoken words, we cast aside.
With every laugh, our souls align,
In moments rare, our hearts entwine.

The universe conspired so,
As through the crowd, our feelings flow.
In serendipity, we take flight,
The world transformed, they feel so right.

Each stolen moment, sweet surprise,
Together lost in wonder's eyes.
No maps required, we pave our way,
In this bright dance, we choose to stay.

So here's to chance, to joy unclaimed,
To every soul whose love we named.
In serendipity's gentle embrace,
We find our home, our sacred place.

Companions in Time

Through seasons change and years unfold,
In every story, our hearts told.
Companions true, through thick and thin,
Together always, we shall begin.

With laughter shared in warm embrace,
We walk this path, a sacred space.
In whispered dreams beneath the stars,
Our souls connect, no distance far.

The clock ticks on, yet we remain,
In joy and sorrow, love is gained.
From dawn to dusk, we hold the light,
With hands united, we'll do what's right.

Each chapter written, memories flow,
Through tides of time, our spirits glow.
As stories weave, our bond grows strong,
In each heartbeat, we find our song.

So here we stand, on life's grand stage,
Companions in time, we write each page.
For in each moment, side by side,
In love, in friendship, we abide.

Shadows and Sunlight

In shadows deep, where secrets lay,
The whispering winds softly sway.
Yet through the dark, a light breaks free,
A dance of hope, for you and me.

The sun will rise, the night will fall,
In every heartbeat, we hear the call.
Through laughter bright, and tears that flow,
In shadows and light, our love will grow.

We wander paths where fears reside,
Yet hand in hand, we still abide.
In every corner, echoes blend,
In shadows cast, on light depend.

Embrace the darkness, cherish the day,
In every moment, come what may.
With shadows dancing, sunlight plays,
Our hearts entwined through twilight's haze.

So let us tread where both reside,
In sunlit dreams, together abide.
For shadows fade, but love stays bright,
In every dawn, we find our light.

The Symphony of Together

In harmony we blend our souls,
Each note a story to behold.
Together we create a sound,
In every heart, a joy profound.

The rhythm of our laughter strong,
Emerging like a timeless song.
With every step we dance in time,
A melody that feels like rhyme.

When shadows lurk, we hold the light,
A symphony in darkest night.
Your voice, a beacon that can steer,
In perfect pitch, I'm always near.

United beats, a steadfast flow,
In every breath, together grow.
A chorus rich, we intertwine,
Together, we are so divine.

As seasons change, our song remains,
Through joy and grief, love never wanes.
In every chord, a promise made,
A symphony that won't evaporate.

Kaleidoscope of Us

Tiny fragments, colors bright,
In every glance, a dance of light.
A tapestry of dreams we weave,
In every moment, we believe.

With shifting patterns, hearts align,
Together in this grand design.
The world's a canvas for our love,
A masterpiece from skies above.

As laughter spills in vibrant hues,
We paint the air in varied views.
Each twist and turn, a new delight,
In kaleidoscope, we take flight.

Reflections of our hopes and fears,
Through every color, joy appears.
In shades of gold and deep indigo,
Together through the highs and low.

You are my prism, pure and true,
Transforming light in all we do.
In every shift, our spirits blend,
Forever more, we transcend.

Uncharted Connections

In worlds unknown, our paths entwine,
Two hearts adrift, by fate we shine.
With open minds, we venture forth,
In every step, we find our worth.

Through unmarked trails where dreams ignite,
We forge ahead, hearts burning bright.
The bonds we build, a sacred trust,
In every challenge, rise we must.

As whispers echo through the trees,
We find our comfort in the breeze.
With hands held tight, we navigate,
A journey woven, never late.

Across the seas, through skies we roam,
In every heartbeat, we find home.
An atlas drawn in love's embrace,
In this vast world, we find our place.

With every twist, our spirits soar,
Uncharted realms, we will explore.
Together strong, our hearts ignite,
In every moment, pure delight.

Made of Dreams

In starlit skies, our hopes reside,
A universe where dreams collide.
With eyes aglow, we chase the night,
Each whisper holds a spark of light.

From fleeting thoughts, we shape our fate,
Together in this dance of late.
With every breath, we craft and scheme,
Our lives a canvas made of dreams.

Through mountains high and valleys low,
In every step, our spirits grow.
The echoes of our laughter cling,
In every note, our voices sing.

With cherished wishes, hand in hand,
We mold our world, a promised land.
In dreams, we find our moments rare,
A sacred bond beyond compare.

In twilight's glow, we dare to dream,
A vision shared, a radiant beam.
With open hearts, we light the way,
In the tapestry of life, we play.

Bridges We Build

With sturdy beams and open hearts,
We forge connections, never apart.
Across the waters, reaching wide,
Together we stand, side by side.

Every plank a story shared,
In laughter and love, we are bared.
A testament to dreams we chase,
In unity, we find our place.

Through storms that shake and winds that roar,
Our bridges hold, they ask for more.
With faith we walk, through shadows cast,
In moments fleeting, our roots hold fast.

From distant shores, we bring our hopes,
In woven paths, our spirit copes.
A tapestry of souls entwined,
In every bridge, a bond defined.

So let us build, with steady hands,
A world where love forever stands.
Where bridges cross and hearts will flow,
In every path, together we grow.

Through Unseen Horizons

Beneath the veil of twilight sky,
We wander forth with dreams to fly.
Each step we take, a silent prayer,
For magic waits, just lurking there.

The stars align, the night unfolds,
A tapestry of stories told.
Through unseen paths, our spirits soar,
We chase the dawn, forevermore.

In whispers soft, the shadows sweep,
As secrets murmur, still and deep.
We listen close, embrace the sound,
In hidden realms, the lost are found.

With every breath, we draw the light,
To pierce the dark, ignite the night.
Together we seek the brave unknown,
Through unseen horizons, we have grown.

So let us venture, hand in hand,
To places where our dreams expand.
Where every dawn brings fresh surprise,
And endless wonders fill our skies.

Navigating the Unknown

With compass set, we leave the shore,
To find the dreams we've never bore.
The map unwritten in our hearts,
In navigating, each new start.

Through waves that crash and winds that twist,
We chase the sun, we can't resist.
With every tide, new paths arise,
In depths of night, we seek the skies.

The stars above, our guiding light,
In darkness deep, they spark our flight.
We trust the journey lies ahead,
In every step, a trace we've led.

The unknown calls with voices soft,
In whispering winds, our spirits loft.
Together we weave through shadowed lands,
With courage strong, we make our plans.

So let us sail on dreams anew,
In boats of hope, in skies so blue.
Navigating through the vast expanse,
With open hearts, we seize our chance.

Merging Trails

In forests deep, where shadows blend,
Our paths converge, we find a friend.
With laughter shared among the trees,
Merging trails, like gentle breeze.

Each step we take, a journey shared,
In silent glades, we've cared and dared.
With every twist, our souls unite,
In harmony, we take our flight.

Through winding paths and mountain high,
Our spirits soar, we touch the sky.
Together we carve a destiny,
In merging trails, we set it free.

The echoes linger in the air,
As nature holds our dreams with care.
In every bend, a tale unfolds,
With shared embrace, our hearts are bold.

So let us wander, side by side,
In every step, our love will guide.
Merging trails, forevermore,
In unity, we will explore.

Heartfelt Expeditions

In whispers soft, we tread the path,
With every step, we feel the math,
Of laughter shared and tears that flow,
A journey forged, together we grow.

Through valleys deep and mountains tall,
We gather strength, we never fall,
In nature's arms, we find our song,
With every heartbeat, we belong.

The stars above, our guiding light,
In darkest hours, they shine so bright,
With open hearts and minds so free,
We seek the truth, just you and me.

Each memory carved, each moment dear,
In the sacred still, we draw you near,
An endless dance, in hope we trust,
Our passion burns, like starlit dust.

As seasons change and time unwinds,
The love we share, the ties that bind,
Forever cherished, in soul and fire,
Our heartfelt journey, a grand desire.

A Voyage of Kindred Spirits

Upon the waves, our spirits rise,
In laughter shared beneath the skies,
With sails unfurled and hearts so wide,
We navigate this wondrous tide.

Through stormy nights and sunny days,
We chart our course in endless ways,
With every ripple, laughter glows,
Together, yes, this love still flows.

With gentle winds, we learn to glide,
In unity, no need to hide,
The compass spins, yet true we stay,
Kindred souls, come what may.

In bonfire light, we share our dreams,
The world unfolds in vibrant themes,
With every tale and whispered prayer,
We find the magic lingering there.

As shores recede and stars ignite,
Our spirits bound in pure delight,
Forever sailing, hand in hand,
Through time and tides, our hearts will stand.

Capturing the Essence

With every brush and stroke of light,
We paint the world in colors bright,
Moments captured, fleeting yet true,
In frames of love, we find the new.

Life's canvas broad, we learn to blend,
Each hue a story, each shade a friend,
From laughter's joy to sorrow's grace,
In every glance, the truth we trace.

Through shadows deep and brightness pure,
We seek the beauty, the heart's allure,
In every portrait, a piece of soul,
Creativity, our perfect goal.

In nature's still, we find our muse,
In quiet moments, we let light fuse,
With every click, we freeze the time,
Capturing essence, pure and sublime.

As seasons change and memories bloom,
We celebrate, dispelling gloom,
With every art, our hearts entwined,
In life's creation, love defined.

Trails in Bloom

Through winding paths our journey flows,
With vibrant blooms, the trail bestows,
Each petal whispers stories old,
Of hope and dreams and hearts of gold.

Beneath the sun, the flowers sway,
Inviting us to pause and play,
In every corner, beauty found,
While nature sings, a soothing sound.

The rustling leaves, a gentle guide,
We walk together, side by side,
In fragrant air, our spirits lift,
Embracing life, this precious gift.

With every step, the joy we share,
In trails of bloom, we breathe the air,
A tapestry of colors bright,
Together navigating light.

As seasons shift and petals fall,
We cherish memories, one and all,
In nature's hug, our hearts will bloom,
Forever bound in love's sweet room.

Portals of Possibility

In shadows where dreams dare to dwell,
Whispers of hope weave their spell.
Each choice a key, unsealed at last,
Unlocks the future, freeing the past.

Through corridors bright, we chase our fate,
In every heartbeat, we navigate.
Visionaries in a land of might,
Together we rise, igniting the light.

Bridges form where the rivers meet,
Soulful connections in every beat.
In the silence, a symphony plays,
Guiding us onward through the maze.

Embrace the magic, let it unfold,
Every story waits to be told.
Venturing forth on the woven skin,
Of possibility, where dreams begin.

With open hearts and hands held high,
We reach for the stars, learning to fly.
In portals of thought, we discover more,
A landscape of wonders, an endless door.

Colliding Stars

In the galaxy's vast, twinkling sea,
Two stars align, like you and me.
With cosmic dance, they spin and sway,
Illuminating paths that light the way.

Gravity pulls, a force so strong,
In the vast expanse where we belong.
Each collision sparks a fiery glow,
Creating worlds for the dreamers to sow.

In the depth of night, we chase our fate,
Wishing on flames that never abate.
Hearts intertwined in celestial play,
Guided by orbits, we find our way.

Together we burn, a radiant flare,
Breaking through darkness, a bond so rare.
In stellar skies, our love ignites,
Colliding hearts in the hush of nights.

Through the firmament, tales are spun,
Of timeless love, forever begun.
In the universe's grasp, we rest,
Two colliding stars, forever blessed.

The Butterfly Effect of Us

A flutter of wings in the gentle breeze,
Sets forth a dance, a chain of keys.
Ripples spread wide, they touch the soul,
Transforming lives, making us whole.

With tender whispers, we change the game,
A spark ignites, never the same.
In every moment, a choice we make,
Winds of change, they swirl and quake.

Each action, large or small, unfolds,
Stories written in timeless golds.
Our laughter echoes, a fleeting sound,
In the vastness, connections are found.

The world spins softly on threads of fate,
As we weave our tale, it's never too late.
With every heartbeat, the future sways,
Bearing witness to the love that stays.

In the dance of life, let's play our part,
Butterflies flutter, where thoughts impart.
Together as one, we'll dare to fly,
In the vast expanse, just you and I.

Through the Canvas of Time

Brush strokes mingle on the canvas wide,
Painting our story, a cherished guide.
With colors bold and shades of soft,
In the gallery of moments, we drift aloft.

Each frame a memory, a tale to tell,
Through whispers of laughter, we weave so well.
In the light of dusk, our visions twine,
Crafting a masterpiece, yours and mine.

Seasons change, yet the art remains,
In vibrant hues, we dance through gains.
Every heartbeat a note in our song,
Through melodies sweet where dreams belong.

In the gallery's heart, we pause to see,
The beauty of life's splendid tapestry.
Through shadows and light, the colors blend,
A narrative flowing, without an end.

With each passing stroke, our spirits soar,
Creating a legacy forevermore.
Through the canvas of time, we are the muse,
In art's embrace, we cannot lose.

Boundless Roads

Winding paths beneath the sky,
Silent whispers, dreams that fly.
Every turn leads somewhere new,
A journey shared, just me and you.

Endless stretches, horizons wide,
Through the valleys, side by side.
Footprints linger on the ground,
In every heartbeat, love is found.

The sun will set, the stars will gleam,
As we chase after every dream.
With courage bright and spirit bold,
These boundless roads have stories told.

As seasons change, and rivers flow,
We'll tread where wildflowers grow.
Hand in hand as shadows blend,
On these roads, our hearts transcend.

Through laughter's echo, tears that fall,
Together strong, we'll conquer all.
Each mile a memory forged with grace,
In boundless roads, we've found our place.

Echoes of Togetherness

In quiet moments, hearts align,
A bond unbroken, yours and mine.
Through storms and calm, we find our way,
In echoes soft, where shadows play.

We share the weight, the joy, the strife,
Through the tapestry we weave, our life.
But in the silence, we hear the sound,
Of love's sweet echo that knows no bounds.

Every laugh, each tear we share,
In the golden light, we're laid bare.
Together strong, through night and day,
In echoes of love, we'll find our way.

From whispered secrets to bold refrains,
Our dream together, all it contains.
The universe signs in cosmic cues,
In echoes of togetherness, we choose.

So here we stand, forever near,
With every heartbeat, love's sincere.
In life's grand song, our voices blend,
In echoes that linger, love will transcend.

Steps Through Starlit Dreams

Underneath the midnight sky,
We take our steps, you and I.
Guided by the silver light,
In starlit dreams, the world feels right.

With every wish, our spirits rise,
Chasing freedom among the skies.
We dance through shadows, hand in hand,
Building castles upon the sand.

Whispers of night in fragrant air,
Together, we find moments rare.
Each twinkle holds a secret shared,
In starlit dreams, we are prepared.

Through lush horizons, far and wide,
In every heartbeat, we confide.
With every step, the night unfolds,
As starlit dreams whisper, "Be bold."

Held by the night, our hearts take flight,
Guided always by love's pure light.
In every breath, a memory gleams,
As we wander through starlit dreams.

Paths Intertwined

In a world of twists and turns,
Through the lessons, love still burns.
Two souls wandering hand in hand,
In paths intertwined, we understand.

Through the seasons, laughter flows,
Shared moments where affection grows.
A dance of fate, a heart's design,
In every step, our lives align.

From quiet dawns to twilight's glow,
In every heartbeat, the truth will show.
Together we walk, through storm and shine,
For our journey's made, in paths entwined.

Through winding trails and hidden ways,
We'll write our story in endless days.
Two hearts as one, forever combined,
A tapestry woven, in paths aligned.

So here we stand, unafraid to soar,
With every challenge, we'll fight for more.
Together forever, no need to define,
In this beautiful dance, our paths intertwined.

Wings of Change

A gentle breeze sweeps through the trees,
Carrying whispers only the heart sees.
With each flutter, new paths we find,
Embracing the shift of the restless mind.

Chasing shadows, we learn to fly,
With dreams as our wings, we touch the sky.
In every ending, beginnings await,
A tapestry woven by fate, not by straight.

Hope hovers softly, a radiant hue,
Guiding us onward, showing what's true.
In the dance of life, we take each chance,
To spread our wings and join the dance.

Through storms we soar, through darkness we glide,
Trusting the journey, with love as our guide.
Each beat of our wings, a pledge to embrace,
The wonder of change, the beauty of grace.

As we rise higher, we shed the old skin,
Casting away doubts that linger within.
With wings open wide, we feel the light,
Together we thrive, we take to flight.

Threads of Time

In the loom of life, the threads intertwine,
Stories of struggle, and moments divine.
Each stitch a memory, a joy or a tear,
Woven with love, a tapestry dear.

The past and the future, a delicate dance,
Echoes of laughter, a fleeting glance.
Through seasons of change, we hold on tight,
To the threads of our dreams, shining bright.

Time whispers secrets in the still of the night,
Each thread a lesson, guiding our flight.
With patience we weave, with courage we find,
A quilt of our stories, uniquely designed.

Moments strung like pearls on a line,
A necklace of memories, a treasure divine.
In the fabric of life, together we tie,
The dreams of today with the hopes that don't die.

As time flows onward, we continue to sew,
The beautiful patterns of life's ebb and flow.
Each thread a reminder, we are not alone,
In the tapestry of time, we have all grown.

The Map to Our Hearts

Beneath the stars, our journey begins,
With paths intertwined like waves on the winds.
We chart our course with dreams as our guide,
Drawing a map where love won't hide.

Each bend in the road tells a story anew,
Of laughter, of tears, and the moments we grew.
With every heartbeat, we step to the beat,
Creating a map that guides our feet.

Through mountains of hope and valleys of fear,
Together we wander, with hearts ever near.
In shadows and light, we navigate fate,
Finding the way to a love that's innate.

As we venture forth, hand in hand,
The map we unfold reveals our land.
Each mark a promise, a bond that won't part,
Leading us lovingly to the map of our hearts.

In every adventure, in moments we share,
The map to our hearts drawn with utmost care.
With each step, we gather the moments unspoken,
A treasure unveiled, no promise unbroken.

Waves of Kindred Spirit

In the ocean of life, we ride on the waves,
Finding our kin in the hearts that it saves.
With every crest, there's a bond that is formed,
Together we rise, together we're warmed.

Through turbulent tides, we stand side by side,
In the depths of the sea, in the ebb and the glide.
With laughter and love, we write our own song,
On waves of kindred spirit, where we all belong.

The rhythm of hearts beats in time with the sea,
Carrying whispers of you and of me.
In currents of trust, our spirits unite,
Navigating through both the dark and the light.

As the waves dance vividly under the sun,
We cherish our moments, two souls become one.
Through the rise and the fall, together we soar,
Riding the waves, forever wanting more.

For when our hearts meet in this vast, wild sea,
We are kindred spirits, forever set free.
Like waves on the shore, let our love never cease,
In the ocean of life, we find our sweet peace.

Milton Keynes UK
Ingram Content Group UK Ltd.
UKHW020038271124
451585UK00012B/916